Solar Subjugation

poems by

Toni La Ree Bennett

Finishing Line Press
Georgetown, Kentucky

Solar Subjugation

Copyright © 2019 by Toni La Ree Bennett
ISBN 978-1-63534-844-6 First Edition
All rights reserved under International and Pan-American Copyright Conventions. No part of this book may be reproduced in any manner whatsoever without written permission from the publisher, except in the case of brief quotations embodied in critical articles and reviews.

ACKNOWLEDGMENTS

The author wishes to acknowledge the publications in which some of these poems first appeared:

Sunrise at the Mall; Sun-Shattered Bird; Solar Subjugation ~ *The Write Launch*
Desert Flesh ~ *Adagio Verse Quarterly*
Sun ~ *Ground Fresh Thursday* (GFT Press)
The Sun is Dying (Again) ~ *Pierian Springs*
Easter Moon ~ *The Raven's Perch, Alexandria Quarterly Review*

Publisher: Leah Maines
Editor: Christen Kincaid
Cover Art: "Burning Man" ©Toni La Ree Bennett, 2018. Previously published in a slightly different version in WomenArts Quarterly, Volume 8, Issue 1 February 2018.
Author Photo: Toni La Ree Bennett, 2018
Cover Design: Toni La Ree Bennett

Printed in the USA on acid-free paper.
Order online: www.finishinglinepress.com
also available on amazon.com

Author inquiries and mail orders:
Finishing Line Press
P. O. Box 1626
Georgetown, Kentucky 40324
U. S. A.

Table of Contents

Part I

Sunrise at the Mall 1
Mall Parking Lot in July 2
Desert Flesh 4
Sun 5
Il Sole Mi Fa Paura 6
Blinded Poet 7
White Skies 9
Sun-Shattered Bird 12
Mind of Fire 13
Solar Subjugation 14
The Sun is Dying (Again) 16

Part II

Dusk 17
There is no Temple 18
Still I Was Lost 20
Inside the Moon 21
Easter Moon 22
So Many Clues 23
Orange Grove in Fog 27
Rainstorm at a Strip Mall in L.A. 28
Il Diluvio 30
Etruscan Well 32
Guess at Essence 33
Earth Arms 34

PART I

Sunrise at the Mall

Twiggy fingers on bare branches
reach for the sky's persimmon skin,
bruised with blue and purple clouds.

An ambulance takes a shortcut through
an empty parking lot, wailing in despair
while a seagull rises in the frigid air

and then swoops low like he's fallen
through a trap door, but he's not flying
anywhere in particular, just showing off.

Mall Parking Lot in July

Once you take that first step
there is no going back.
But if you follow the arrows,
you're going in circles.
Faded arrows leading to more arrows
that lead you astray. Yellow diagonal lines
lead to more diagonal lines going
the opposite direction. Nothing for it

but to keep moving forward
and always the same view
in the morning with the gently tentative sun
lighting the left side of your face
as you travel south
and in the afternoon, the brilliantly blasé sun
scorching the left side of your face
as you travel north. As you travel on your way,
hot neon signs always silently offer you the same
things: **FOOD   MASSAGE   SHOES   BOOKS.**

The husks of temporarily abandoned cars
huddle together in their metal graveyard
waiting to claim your bones if you linger;
even the temperature-controlled
oasis where their owners are idling,
a place of coolness, sustenance, and soothing music,
is as much of a wasteland. There is no relief there.
You know, by the slow-moving shadows
projected in silhouette on the asphalt,
that birds are up there somewhere

but you would be blinded if you looked
for them. It is enough to know
they are up there. There is no shelter,
not even from the sliver of shade
created by the three-eyed metal lampposts
that might be communicating with aliens.

A cheeseburger wrapper blows across the lot
like a tumbleweed pushed by a sultry, sulking wind
and as you watch it move across your path
you jump back in fear of your double shadow

coming up fast behind you. You quicken
your steps, knowing that only by moving
will you ever escape but the hundredth step
feels just as futile as the first.
And yet it is not. There will be that one step
that takes you through this urban desert
to the other side. A step no different
than any of the others that came before.

Desert Flesh

I felt a winter urge to go
to Mexico, and darken into palm.

As my blood percolated at a low boil,
and my body carved its impression in the sand,
I felt a shape climb me like a rock.
I knew that inside this sordid skin,
luscious language was being incubated
that did not produce any shadow,
being all shadow.

At first, the flesh resisted, then the
rolling stomach yielded to my fingers,
the way a woman must feel to a man.

The exotic palette of his rippling hide
shimmered with church bells,
watermelons, crusty seahorses,
and the lurid beaks of parrots, all blended
into a cryptic smear randomly applied
with a delicate, delirious knife. At first, I feared

this body heavy with the scent of dragon.
But, seduced into piety by the power of his steady,
languid stare, I realized that in this deep place,
I was nothing more than a milky whisper to him.

And then he was gone, like the enormous rain.

Sun

A father on a bus holds the baby
close to his chest.

As the bus rattles over a bridge,
a shaft of sunlight melts through
the window, anointing the child.

The father, thinking he knows
what to do, shields the baby's
face with one huge hand.

The baby, till now docile
and pliable in his father's embrace,
jerks his head so that it falls back
into the patch of sunlight.

Someday,
he would forgive his father even this.

Il sole mi fa paura

Il sole mi fa paura
anche la piazza vuota.

É una lunga strada
attraverso la piazza
sotto il sole scottante.

*The sun frightens me
also the empty piazza.*

*It's a long way
across the piazza
under the burning sun.*

Blinded Poet

On the way to the reading, the poet is blinded—

    blinded by oncoming headlights
    by flashing red and green in the crosswalk,
    by neon signs on storefronts, blinded
    by the candle on the wooden table

at the pretentious little bar
where the reading is taking place.

The next day, on her way to a workshop
led by a famous poet in town for the weekend
she shields her face with an arm raised
against the sun and once inside,
puts on a visor
to keep the ceiling lights at bay
leaving her sunglasses on
to dampen the brightness
infiltrating tissue-thin eyelids.

Closing her eyes as she reads
her memorized poem,
her body contracts, recoiling
from the metaphoric spotlight
she's put herself into.

Each student explains
what her poem means
to them,
and her words start multiplying
like zealous cells,
dividing into many different
poems, none of which are *her* poem.

She listens half-heartedly, the sounds
arriving ever more faintly as she leans
back into the musty armchair, letting
her muscles loosen while she watches
the glowing afternoon
tranquilized by subtle dusk.

White Skies

White skies
        pressing down like a pillow
                slowly pushed on your face by a calm killer

White skies
        as pale as the skin of your bloodless body
                discovered among rotting reeds

*****

It matters what direction
the wind is coming from
more than ever.

Birds have been falling from the skies
for two weeks and still the skies are white
with smoke
from fire and fury
creeping in from the north—
smoky clouds shaped like gnarled fingers.

The sun—
our nuclear reactor friend—
is eclipsing, sidelined
by the fire spreading on
the planet's surface.

And the temperatures rise
whether one believes in them or not;
even the unbelievers sweat
as if the molten core were seeping
through the surface.

Everyone is praying for a south wind
to pull the smoke back
from whence it came
but there is no wind at all
only the slowly gathering smoke
surrounding us as we huddle
behind our covered wagons,
windows closed and fans
circulating dead, used up air.

As each day's weather report
is consulted, we wonder if this will be
the day the south winds come.
But the projection is still smoke.
Always smoke.
Forever smoke.
No one has to see the fire
to know it's real.
The spectacle of white skies from all sides
is enough to make us believe.

*****

A woman, brave or foolish enough
to go outside, stands in the middle
of a deserted park, watching
a teasing patch of blue emerge and then
a silver wisp of smoke erasing it.
For a few moments,
her upraised head had hoped.

Now a SW wind does a little dance
but is soon suppressed.
The woman turns east,
then south, then west, seeing nothing

but white skies. She gathers
her courage and turns to the north
to face the slowly rolling smoke
before giving up and going inside.

With no wind, there is only silence.
The silence of the planet's people
holding their breath, trying to
preserve their lungs to breathe
another day. Not daring to speak
for fear of giving the fire fuel.

One bird has come back
from the dead,
her companions drowned
while seeking relief
from the smoke and the fire and the fury.

And yet this one bird survives.
Will one be enough?
Enough to drop a seed on
a blasted patch of earth,
to be the instrument
bringing seed to earth,
for a fertile meeting
that will engender a new world?

But with whom shall she mate
now
all the other birds are gone?

Sun-Shattered Bird
> *[The most probable fate of the planet is absorption by the Sun in about 7.5 billion years..."* —Wikipedia]

One small mistake in timing,
and now a bird is just a small clump
in the street. I was hoping it was a leaf.

Such a small mistake, costing more than
everything. She should have made it.
All she needed was a quick climb
over the oncoming car.
Stupid stupid such a stupid bird—
you're supposed to know better.

But as I start lethargically jogging
my way back home, I humbly realize
my sunglasses are no match
for the hallelujah light
that makes me stumble
and fall to my knees.

I realized it had not been her fault
but the sun's—that sun
that sneaks closer every day,
melting us so slowly
we feel only slightly softer, nothing

to be alarmed about. But on this day,
the sun sent a quicksilver messenger
from its flaming core
blinding the bird with a shard of light,
dooming her to one final flight.

As I shield my eyes and stumble
down the street, I vow not to be placated
by magic crop-growing tricks
or sultry tanned and cancerous bodies.
I curse the dragon star,
knowing that it burns to absorb us all.

Mind of Fire
    (after Wallace Stevens)

One must have a mind of fire
to watch the sun turn solids into liquid
and bake the green land to brown;

and have been sweltering for eons
to watch the desert eat the forest mile by mile,
the pines dropping their needles

like ballistic missiles from the sky; and not to blink
at the dessicated lizard on the rock,
in a canyon bled of water,

which is the promised land
full of broken promises to ourselves
that flutter down from skyscrapers like confetti.

For the traveler, roasting his skin on the last beach
nothing through thick sunglasses beholds—
the nothing that was coming and the nothing that will be.

Solar Subjugation
August 21, 2017

Today, at key locations in a diagonal swath
across the United States
people cheered both
the disappearance and reappearance
of the sun. Their collective throats
bellowed at the absorption of the light
and then erupted *en masse* at the victory
over the black disk that hid it from us.

Everyone wanted to be covered
by the path of totality today
even though the resonance of that word
in a time of tyrants, dictators, and the threat
of nuclear war is not lost on anyone.

Everyone wanted to be disoriented,
flung into a day-time darkness,
chilled in the middle
of a hot summer day,
reminded of our ant-like existence.
Everyone wanted to see nature up-ended,
to feel the relief that a cosmic
hide and seek game could give.

We pat ourselves on the back at knowing more
than our ancestors; we know the sun is coming
back and yet we still cheer in amazement
at its return because we know too well that anything
can happen. We have set things in motion
and know that dominoes will fall.
At a time when we should be celebrating
our assurance that the sun will return,
we know that it might not.

And as eons pass, our descendants, if we have any,
will look back at our broadcasts and streaming
and twitters and posts and smile wistfully
at our childish excitement. As soon as it was over
we started counting down the days to the next one
so we could see it all over again.

But the time of eclipses is winding down.
Our descendants will yearn for the return
of the days in which a slow-motion
marshmallow moon could completely
cover the never-blinking face of a flaming goddess,
which daily dares us to look her in the eye.

The Sun is Dying (Again)

Dusk is supposed to be languorous
        bleaching the pigment-saturated day sanable
when all we are able to determine

is the proclivity for solids to wax porous
        when every object tags its double
each shadow a shocking sermon

of what will become of us
        when the earth exerts its final pull
and then…the shocking drop of the sun.

I counted on you, peroxide
        hussy to incubate my halcyon
dreams of a dependable origin.

But instead of the ox-eyed
        drudge I counted on, you splashed neon
before dropping into an invisible coffin.

Knowing this is not the first time you have died,
        yet daunted by the improbability of another dawn,
I sink to my knees, gut-punched by your sinking grin.

PART II

Dusk

Stand in the front door
at dusk; you must bring your
own destination.

Bats waiting for night.
Walking on their wings—nubby,
webbed crutches.

Beyond obvious
beauty, fur may even be
capable of thought.

You regret the fact
that your skin has never
had a chance to fly.

There is no Temple

The iron gate butlers me
inside, knowing how futile
my search for an ancient goddess will be.

My hopeful feet stumble
on an empty pack of Diana-brand cigarettes.

A message from above?
I can smell her musky amusement
wafting down from La Rocca.

Misleading paths roller-coaster me
around instead of up…

cradled in an armful of stone,
a batrachian basin reflects nothing back—
here, you must bring your own double.

Here, there are only holes in stone
framing heavy air that darkens
with a chuckle

expecting me to panic.

There is only a hawk who tells me
not here, not here; try there, not there
always on some higher hill, the hope.

I will not leave until I've stumbled
over the hem of your gown.

Tu—sei qui, girlfriend?

Every pile of rocks looks like your temple—
looks nothing like a temple.

Impotent, crippled architecture
begins to hum a lullaby
expecting me to sleep with ruins tonight.

But the butler shuts down at dusk
so I aim myself like an arrow
and sail over heart-breaking stones
into the pink and grey of a dying day.

I hoped to at least come back
with a revelation in my pocket
but all I have is this empty
pack of cigarettes.

Which is pretty much
the same thing.

> *There is no temple.*
> *It is all temple.*

Still I Was Lost

I was lost

seven hills surrounding me;
their names I could not say
for I was lost,

lost, not for the first time

lost again

standing on a Roman bridge
nothing stronger
nothing lasts longer
stone arching triumphantly
over the city's liquid map

when the hunched shoulders
of an imperial bird plunged me
into deep shadows under
outspread wings, at the mercy

of unrelenting talons
gripping concrete, his bulk
backed by a seamless blue sky
slowly veering to violet.

As he pointed the way with
autocratic beak,
still I stood, directionless,
not knowing if this gesture
was a direction
or a deterrent

and still I was lost.

Inside the Moon

Once more you journey to the first star,
your body arriving as liquid light,
swallowed into a dark spot.
Again you tunnel through to the other
side, opening yourself to the flaying
sun. You know once again what it is

to be reflective, incapable
of generating your own heat.
What frightening dependence.

Should you return, I will beg you,
this time, to remember your ability
to sway the direction of your own heavy seas,
to control the pulse of your own planet.

Easter Moon

On this day before Easter,
the two of us have found a lake
to attach ourselves to on our last trip
together. What is it about the edge
of water that draws one to its side?

I watch a swan on the lake with her young
while you forage for wood.
That night, with only the campfire to
embrace me, I wait until you go
inside our cave on wheels and then

I belly down to the ground,
brace myself against a rock,
steadying my well-traveled Pentax
and point my 35mm eye at the sky.
While the wobbly image

of the full moon floats in the middle
of the lake, mocking me,
I make a pitiful attempt to bring this Easter
eve moon home as a souvenir.
As the sun takes the moon's place

on Easter morning, I wonder
what I'm doing in New Zealand
instead of being home in Seattle
with my son. As I hand you
a chocolate egg, I feel the small

satisfaction of a reflected event.
It isn't the moon, but it's something.

So Many Clues

The white bird shivers
and waits to find out
if she will die.
Or not.

The spider crawls to a place
he has no business being.

From under the bushes
the moaning won't stop.

It started so suddenly.
I wonder
if the door is locked.

This is the most dangerous business
I've ever been about;
and of course the moon,

not a bit ashamed,
hunches over the tiny
unmarked grave.

There is not enough light;
there will be no witnesses.
The light has burnt out;
the fuses are blown.

Only a flashlight with weak batteries
left and still the white bird shivers,
leaving a fragile feather
where it has no business being.

The spider is moaning—
what is the moon doing in my lap?
I thought I checked all the doors.
I have no business moaning.

The shedding of feathers
has only just begun;
poor bird will be naked soon
with nothing but the cold moon
to spotlight her disgrace.

Under the bushes, you can't see it;
don't try looking, but it's there

just outside the window
on the other side of the door.
I hope the door is locked.

I can't stop shivering;
I might live through it.

The spider perches on the pillow
framed by a light
from someone else's window

next to an incongruous feather
left on purpose
to incite a confession.

I'm not admitting anything.
I have no business being here;
this business might end badly.

There is no way to bury it;
the moaning keeps rising
from that same place.

Don't dig it up again;
that hunger is none of your business—
the hunger
that will not, can not,
has not, ever been sated.

From the grave it leaks
under the locked door.
I can't remember
if I locked the door.

Evidence is building.

I have drunk and seen
the spider;
if I leave that last drop
maybe the moon will stop moaning.

The spider under the bushes is shivering;
wine spills in unreadable patterns
on the snow of white feathers.

The moaning bird mourns her loss;
who would have thought the bird
would have had so many feathers.

The spider may or may not
be at the bottom of the glass;
there is not enough light to find out.
All the threads belong to one web.

The curdled cries
bruit the unburied crime;
save a feather to mark the grave.

A wine-stained corpse
shivers just outside the door.
I think the door is locked.

The white bird knows
the door was never locked.

Can there be more than
one conclusion
with so many clues?

Orange Grove in Fog

Cocooned in fog, an orderly army
of gray-legged trees wait in patient formation,
perturbed with a million embryonic suns,
capped by bouffant viridescence,
constructing a canopy over a self-sufficient galaxy,
stretching their branches like eager fingers
across the crooked swath of a divisive path
reaching lustily for each other's woody touch—
symmetry plotting to go seasonally mad.

Rainstorm at a Strip Mall in L.A.

You've never said anything more true
than the sound of those raindrops
in your video on Facebook.

You sent a ten-second slice of your life
through the Facebook door—
the only one you keep open.

All you say is that it's raining in L.A.
You say it with an exclamation mark;
you're too mature for emoticons.

Or emotionless.

I play this video over and over
in a darkened room, avoiding
the sun I moved up north to escape,
wanting rigid demarcations of the past
smeared by fog, mist, snow. And rain.

Now you tease me with this
pattering of rain on a car roof.
Some drops explode on the metal
while others drum delicately
on the surface over your head.

I know to you, the tattoo must sound
like bullets pinging against a tank
or meteors banging into the skin
of a spaceship headed for Mars.

But this is just a random mall
somewhere in L.A.
I don't know if you are alone.
I only know you are sheltered.
We both know what a thin slice
is protecting you. Like the battered metal
of the Band Aid box you used to bury your fish.

Weather that is not supposed to happen
is always the fiercest.
The temperature in Vegas is not overwhelming
since it's expected; the same temperature
in Seattle wounds by its aberration.

But this is not a weather report you've sent.
And even though it's out there on the Internet
for 857 of your closest friends to see
I'm the only one who can read the message.

By the time I gather the courage to answer
this storm will have passed.
As I put on my sunglasses
and brace for another scorching day,
I keep hearing those rain drops
hurtling down on you,
sitting somewhere in a strip mall in L.A.

Il Diluvio

It started so quietly
boxing us in quickly
while we weren't looking—

were looking in the camera
at what might have been Rome,
might have been home.

It looked like Rome but
one can never be sure.
We don't belong here.

Our apartment is new
is unfinished
is falling apart.

It's a cunning flood;
it can afford to be subtle.
It snuck up on us

while we were looking at the wrong things
while we were distracted by history
while our backs were turned.

The drops started accumulating
while I was offering you
a quartered lemon on a white plate.

We didn't listen to the silence.
We were busy stroking statues
and gazing at each other in antique mirrors.

The nightingales have flown
the courtyard has emptied
the stars are sputtering out

the water is sheeting every street—
swallowing every ambition
every avenue of escape.

All landmarks are disappearing;
parked cars are liquefied
into abstraction. All land looks

the same when covered by water.
We are here to stay. We should
never have come. I've given up

looking for you. I'm going for help.
My feet no longer touch the ground.
I'm submerged and spinning farther

and farther away from you. Or closer.
I can't tell. My last words to you bubble
to the top, wobbling desperately

on the surface—inarticulate as ever.

Etruscan Well

Ancient opening

like the inside of a worm
all gut

eviscerated skin
as raw as an infant
dripping afterbirth

wounded walls
like a dying gladiator
reluctantly bleeding
into the abyss.

Guess at Essence
    (Lascaux, France)

Everything has
        disappeared
in the dark except

me and this wall.
        Seen fitfully through
spasmodic flames

from the guttering fire,
        the forms dance like
a frantic rubbing taken

from the dark horse of the psyche.
        It is all I have,
this painted wall.

All I have left are these
        smudged colors striding
this uneven, rugged terrain.

Such coarse markings
        coating walls of earth—
only a crude approximation.

This painted wall is merely
        my guess at essence,
seen dimly through smoke-filled eyes.

Earth Arms
(Syracuse, Sicily)

Round stones. Alone,

they fill the aching hollow of my hand;
massed together, they press me to my essence.
There is nothing that can come so near as darkness.

Condemned to cast no more shadows,
I must live with the lack of stars,
except for the sudden eyes of a frantic panther.

Like a proud beggar refusing alms,
I huddle over a dying fire,
sputtering out life in little tongues.

Fondling the walls of the cave like a lover,
I hold one hand out toward the emptiness,
anticipating solidity where it does not exist.

There are no defining edges, only this sliver
in the skin of the earth soothing me
like no lighted place ever could.

Throwing myself onto the cool blanket of earth
I reject the harsh outline of things
from a past that no longer matters.

Suddenly, like buried seeds that gorge themselves
on rain and then explode into light, I am released.
Withered by the shock of unexpected light

I will remember the balm of that dark place.

Toni La Ree Bennett started her writing career as a freelance news correspondent and magazine article writer, later transitioning to literary works. Her poems, stories, articles, memoirs, and photographs have been published in many literary journals, newspapers, and magazines, including *Cimarron Review, Pedestal, Stoneboat, Puerto del Sol, Society of Classical Poets, Hawaii Pacific Review, Gravel, Viet Nam Generation, Memoir Magazine,* and *great weather for MEDIA*. Three of her poems were published in the anthology *The Muse Strikes Back: A Poetic Response by Women to Men* (Story Line Press, 1997) where women writers respond to famous male poets. She has finished three novels, but prefers shorter forms.

She went to college late in life, earning a B.A. in Italian, Ph.D. in English, a professional certificate in Editing, and a professional certificate in Photography. She studied with Mary Ellen Mark in Oaxaca, Mexico and has had numerous photography exhibitions in Seattle. She has been an Acting Instructor at her alma mater, teaching English composition, children's literature, and drama as literature as well as assisting in the preparation of a Medieval drama anthology for publication. She was able to combine her love and knowledge of Adobe software by editing three software tutorial books, and has also done freelance editing for a variety of clients.

For five years, she ran her own publishing company, *Uccelli Press*, designing the book covers and editing books of poetry and short stories. At the same time, she founded and edited *Branches*, an online literary art/writing journal, pairing each literary work with a visual one. Her inspiration comes from world travels as well as quotidian moments. She has recently finished compiling a full-length book of poetry exploring the dichotomy between the sacred and profane places she has visited.

She is the mother of two grown and endlessly creative twin sons and lives with a flock of feisty finches in Seattle, who are providing material for a fourth novel.

www.ingramcontent.com/pod-product-compliance
Lightning Source LLC
LaVergne TN
LVHW040117080426
835507LV00041B/1289